BARRY SCRAPYARD IN THE LATE 1970s AND EARLY 1980s

GEOFF BARKER AND DAVID HOLLAND

AMBERLEY

Acknowledgements

Profound thanks go to my co-author David Holland, for being the instigator and inspiration for this book and for sharing the load in its compilation; Alain Guignet in Lalinde, Dordogne, France, for the slide digital transfers and prints restoration; and my wonderful, ever-patient wife Ann and our children for always accepting that we never went 'straight home'.

Geoff Barker

For Ann, Jane, Nicola, Wendy and Sean.
And the late David Lloyd Victor ('Dai') Woodham MBE, without whom…

First published 2025

Amberley Publishing
The Hill, Stroud
Gloucestershire, GL5 4EP

www.amberley-books.com

ISBN 978 1 3981 1660 3 (print)
ISBN 978 1 3981 1661 0 (ebook)

British Library Cataloguing in Publication Data.
A catalogue record for this book is available from the British Library.

Typesetting by SJmagic DESIGN SERVICES, India.
Printed in Great Britain.

Introduction

I grew up in the 1950s/early 1960s in a terraced house in Harlesden, North West London, with a tiny garden that backed onto a double-tracked line, which ran down from Neasden to Old Oak. Originally the Midland Railway, there was once a small station, which closed in 1902. However, the line was a strategic one for freight and still functions as that today. It was busy all week with BR steam workhorses passing up and down. I remember Standard classes, Austerity Qs, numerous Jintys, the occasional 9F and, once, the bizarre sight of a Garratt. Standing at the fence, I watched those grubby locos hauling wagon trains of coal, steel, cable drums, timber and, occasionally, livestock. A special treat was FA Cup final day, when the line was used as passenger relief, taking football supporters to Wembley Stadium. This brought an incredible array of 'foreign' locos passing our house hauling long trains of fans, hanging out of the windows, waving and whirling wooden rattles, in their scarves, hats and rosettes (no replica shirts then). In those days, as teams making the final generally came from 'up north', there was the amazing spectacle of Black Fives, Jubilees, Coronations, Royal Scots, B1s, A3s and, the most stunning of all to me, the A4 'streaks', ultra-rare sights for this part of London.

These youthful memories come from the years just prior to the Beeching era, which saw the army of BR locos sent to cutters' torches at scrapyards across the country, despite many having decades of life left in them. I always took them for granted, thinking they would be around forever, only bothering to take a handful of black and white pictures with the family Brownie as they passed by. Little did I know that by the end of the decade they would have totally disappeared from our lines – and our lives (or so I thought).

As the 1960s became the 1970s, I was married with three young daughters and obsessed with music and playing guitar. Steam had gone and I had no interest (at that time) in those blue, fume-emitting metal boxes that now pulled the trains of Britain.

By the mid-1970s we had moved to Surrey and I discovered the just-emerging Mid-Hants 'Watercress Line', near Alton, where there was some track and rolling stock. The original MHR line had escaped Beeching, but was closed by BR in 1973. Its new life came in 1975 with the private purchase of the track bed between Ropley and Alresford. We made regular Sunday family trips there. The star attraction was West Country class 4-6-2 No. 34016 *Bodmin*. It arrived at the Watercress in 1976 and it became a joy to watch the restoration gradually progressing. We joined the *Bodmin* 'supporters club' and made donations towards the work, along with buying photos, car stickers and books. We were proud to have played a small part when a magnificently restored *Bodmin* steamed again in 1979. I had no idea what had happened to the loco since the Beeching axe had fallen, but found it had been withdrawn by BR in 1964 and sent to a scrapyard in South Wales – 'Woodham Brothers' at a place called Barry.

On one of our Watercress line visits, I bought a pamphlet produced by the Barry Steam Loco Action Group (BSLAG). It was a total revelation to read about this amazing place and see photographs of the lines of steam locos, just quietly rusting away. We had to have a family trip to South Wales!

Dai Woodham was born in 1919 and worked in the family dock-portering business founded by his great grandfather at the turn of the nineteenth century. Set on the coastline, 10 miles west of Cardiff, Barry Docks had become a key place for South Wales coal exports. In the 1930s, Dai turned to road transport and then into something that would later play a pivotal role in the steam railways of Britain – scrap metal.

Apart from the total disposal of BR's steam fleet, Beeching's Modernisation Plan also demanded a massive reduction in rolling stock. This happened at several locations across the UK and in 1957, Woodham's yard started dismantling railway wagons. However, the scrapping of 16,000 steam locos proved way beyond BR's internal resources, so thousands were sold to private scrapyards. The first to arrive at Barry were four GWR 2-6-0s (Nos 5312, 5360, 5392 and 5397) in 1959. Being in South Wales, the early years saw almost exclusively ex-GWR locos being cut, but such was the volume arriving that not all were scrapped immediately and they began to be stored in sidings at the docks. In 1964, the first Southern locos appeared, including the mighty Bulleid 4-6-2s (one of course being *Bodmin*). During 1965, the destruction of steam locos there was virtually halted. This was not out of any sentiment, but simply that the increasing numbers of wagons, and now brake vans, were far easier to cut. So the locos just sat in their lines, until, as Dai presumed, the wagon supplies dried up.

Between 1959 and 1968, Woodham's bought 297 locos, only cutting eighty. By now, steam preservation groups across the UK had found this new source for locos and the first to depart for safety was LMS 4F 0-6-0 No. 43924 in September 1968.

The 1970s saw large numbers leaving. Locos would be reserved with Dai, whilst funds were raised for their purchase and weekend working parties arrived at Barry, starting preliminary restoration. Only charging the scrap value of each and even allowing payment by installments, but with a theft problem, Woodham's removed brass and copper items for storage until sale. Thefts increased, with major components being stolen and locos even being seriously damaged when enthusiasts used cutting gear to remove parts. All this was done with no regard for the potential owners. So, in 1981, Dai introduced a total ban on weekend working parties.

The early departures were, as they came in, by rail, but with diesel haulage to their new home. However, as the locos deteriorated, much due to salty sea-air exposure, they became unsafe for BR's main lines and low-loaders had to be used. Also, as locos needed to be moved around there were often derailments and with no re-railing facilities, Woodham's were forced to cut wheels. One famous case was GWR 4-6-0 No. 6023 *King Edward II*. In total, 213 locos left the yard for preservation, the last being GWR 2-6-2T No. 5553 in January 1990, after twenty-eight years there. Truly the end of an era, which was compounded when, sadly, Dai Woodham passed away following a battle with cancer in 1994.

In 1979, my wife, Ann, and myself took our three daughters for the first of several summer holidays to a caravan park on Cardigan Bay in West Wales. The drive from Surrey was straightforward – down the M4, over the Severn Bridge and up through Brecon to Newquay.

The return was a little different, involving a deviation before leaving Wales: the long-awaited Barry family trip! That July, Jane (thirteen), Nicola (ten) and Wendy (seven) were told we wouldn't be going straight home and not really knowing exactly where Woodham's was, I just headed to Barry Island. On the elevated road going across, I saw an amazing view to our left: line after line of rusting buffer-to-buffer steam locos.

After some time in the amusement park in Barry, it was down to the yard itself. The first close-up sighting was profound: these giants of steam, steel boiler claddings hanging open exposing asbestos, skeletons of cabs stripped of all parts, smokebox doors, some face-painted, some missing, gardens growing inside, the graffiti of preservation-society names, phone numbers and warnings not to steal parts, sale dates and optimistic relocation sites, hand-painted numbers and famous names, mountains of wheels, wagon parts, in fact, total scrapyard dereliction everywhere. All was set in an eerie silence, which even the amusement-park rides didn't penetrate. An hour here would never be long enough and eventually would run to three or four. Our girls got to enjoy the yard and despite always asking their Mum, 'are we going straight home?', now look back fondly on walking the tracks and climbing in and on the locos (their little brother, Sean, arrived in 1981 and he was taken on later trips too). Nicola is today married to my co-author, David, living within sight and sound of the Swanage Railway, where they often travel behind locos she once clambered on as a little girl, forty years earlier! Apart from my slides and photographs, I have one treasured souvenir: an old leather fireman's glove, hidden inside a cab – I just wish I'd noted which one.

Woodham's yard was an incredible phenomenon and I'm so glad my family and I were able to experience it. The place where the elephants went to die, or not, as over half of UK-preserved locos today are ex-Barry.

I took these photographs on my Pentax ME Super using Fuji black and white and colour slide film, plus some colour print. They were taken across several family holidays, plus a one-day 'Barry Bash' as the yard was running down. I hope you enjoy them as much as I do.

Geoff Barker

On our first visit in 1979 I didn't know Woodham's location, just Barry Island. I'll never forget driving our Ford Transit Camper across to there, when one of our girls said, 'Trains, Dad!' I looked left and saw this incredible view, and it was even more full then.

A shower of rain gives the locos a nice sheen. A great variety is seen here, but an honourable mention for 2-6-2T No. 4115, which now no longer exists. Leaving in 2000, it provided parts for several other locos, until the frames were scrapped at Tyseley in 2016 – but just who was Alfred?

If ever a Barry loco symbolised the squandering of public resources from the 'Beeching plan', it must be Black Five 4-6-0 No. 44901. Arriving in the yard in 1966, only twenty years after construction, it remained there for forty-seven years. Currently, restoration plans are with the Gloucestershire Warwickshire Railway.

Of all my photos, this sums up Barry for me. Line upon line, buffer to buffer, of locos, box cars, brake vans and even a diesel shunter. For an example of how much loco shunting Woodham's undertook, compare the positions of Nos 80072 and 35022 here with the previous colour pictures.

Left: A scene of what seems like total scrapyard chaos, but probably wasn't. I'm sure this view from the houses in the distance did little to aid property sales, unless 'would suit rail enthusiast' was added to the details (I'd have been happy!). It is possibly 9F 2-10-0 No. 92207 in the foreground.

Below: Another elevated shot to show just how packed Woodham's was, even by the mid-1980s. It was often disorientating to walk down the lines when attempting to photograph everything. I often thought, 'have I been down here?'

Same day, more climbing. These are what I called 'where the elephants go to die' photos. Happily, by this time, of course, they didn't. Even huge restorations, such as GWR 4-6-0 *King Edward II* (far right) sitting there with cut wheels, leaving for Didcot in 1984 and steaming again in 2011.

This is 1980 and another cab-roof shot, this time from the top of 2-8-0 No. 2861. At Barry from 1963, this one has an historic place in the story of Woodham's, being the last to leave in 2013, albeit a total wreck. Stripped down at the Llangollen Railway, it provided parts for several other preservation projects.

Left: These perspective views of the lines were quite a sight. Health and safety regulations were flagrantly disregarded for a cab-roof shot – it was 1981! This was the year of Charles and Diana's wedding, so I clipped a portable TV onto our camper-van battery for Ann and the girls to watch.

Below: A study of steam power in black and white. A grim day (which was rare on our trips) as a three-car DMU makes its way across to Barry Island station – 'Alight here for the amusement park'. The kids had enjoyed the yard and the park and were now ready to head home.

There's another book to be made of all the graffiti on Barry locos. 4MT 2-6-4 No. 80098 has the sad (but polite) appeal not to remove any more parts. Not cannibalised, after leaving in 1983 it underwent massive restoration, re-steaming in 1998. No. 4979 *Wootton Hall* waited another three years to depart.

I took this view as, with a bit of suspended reality, it looked like Churchward 2-8-0T No. 4248 was having the smokebox cleared prior to departure with a goods train. Another long-term Woodham's resident, it arrived in 1963 and departed in 1986. Today, it is preserved and on static display at Swindon Steam Railway Museum.

Woodham's could be so peaceful. In July 1981, a glorious summer afternoon, our holiday has ended and the girls are at the amusement park with their mum. Nature is taking over the abandoned wheels as No. 80072 rubs smokeboxes with MN 4-6-2 No. 35022 *Holland America Line*. It departed in 1986 for Swanage and is currently unrestored.

In late autumn 1987, the setting sun mixes with rust and red oxide paint. As can be seen from the foreground, everything rail was scrapped at Woodham's, including 2-8-0 GWR Churchward No. 3862, 4MT 2-6-0 No. 76077 and 2-8-0 GWR Churchward No. 2874.

Seen here with fellow Churchwards, Nos 4253 and 5552 and Black Five No. 73096, a truly dilapidated 2-6-2T, No. 5553, became a celebrated part of the Barry story as the last loco to leave in January 1990 and the longest resident, spending almost twenty-eight years by the seaside. It steamed again in 2002.

A line of (eventually) immaculate again locos stood sentinel over a scene of scrapyard chaos: wagon springs, wooden beams, iron rods and even a porter's trolley – no doubt a collectable today. MN No. 35011 stands with Black Five No. 73156 and GWR No. 5576.

It's 1983 and a more atmospheric monochrome. I can still smell the oil and grease that this photo exudes. With all the junk and debris, it could have seen a massive crowd just passing through. The 150th loco to leave, in 1984, GWR 4-6-0 No. 4953 *Pitchford Hall* steamed again in 2004.

Four years on and much has changed. No. 34072 is still in the same place but would leave that November. All aspects of Barry are here – brake and freight wagons awaiting the torch, locos 'to go' and a pile of scrap. Some of my favourite Barry shots were in evocative black and white.

'I Walk the Line'. In August 1980 I took a wander between the packed lines. BB 4-6-2 No. 34072 *257 Squadron* – seemingly project impossible – left in 1984, steamed in 1990 and later was a joy to see at Swanage with co-author David and his wife (our daughter, Nicola), who clambered on it back then.

In the mid-1980s, it was a surprise to arrive and find the yard fenced, which was installed for safety and security reasons, as theft of parts was still a problem to the end. Compared with the next shot, the thinning out is plain to see, with many locos now gone.

A stop-end buffer view of 8F 2-8-0 No. 48173, Standard class 4MT 2-6-0 No. 76084 and Churchward 2-8-0T No. 4253 on an overcast day in an overgrown yard.

A 1980 study in rust, the regular first view for many years on arrival at Barry. On the left is GWR 2-6-2T No. 5538 and on the right is MN 4-6-2 No. 35011 *General Steam Navigation*, which was sold. Departing in 1983, today there is a unique plan to un-rebuild, restoring the original air-smoothed casing.

In late autumn 1987, the setting sun glows on the woodwork of two brake vans. In the foreground, shaded but vibrant, is 4MT 2-6-4 T No. 80072. 'Going home/1988' was not optimism. It left the yard that July, going home to Wales and the Llangollen Railway, where it steamed once again in 2009.

A contrast in survivability, August 1980. A 1960s Rover 2000 languishes before (from left to right) Churchward 2-8-0 T No. 2807, Churchward 2-8-0T No. 4277, BR class 5MT 4-6-0 No. 73156 and Bulleid MN class 4-6-2 No. 35009 *Shaw Savill*, which had sat in the yard since before the car left the factory. The Rover went unrestored.

More destruction and desolation: nature would quickly reclaim the terrain at Barry wherever there was inactivity. I don't recall seeing many of those box-car freight carriages in the yard. This one was butted up against an enormous pile of discarded wheels. Not much of a picture postcard for a seaside resort.

The absolute end of the line, just fortunately not a loco. This is the burning remains of one of the many brake vans that came to the yard, alongside wheels just randomly lying where they were torched. It is a scene reminiscent of some kind of avant-garde brutalist art exhibition.

Rural Woodham's on a summer's day in the 1980s, looking across the locos towards Barry town. I always wondered what the people in those houses thought of their view. Seeing this again whilst preparing the book was a revelation – there's the camera tripod I left behind! I never noticed that before.

Churchward 2800 class 2-8-0 No. 2807 is by far the oldest locomotive to be rescued from Barry. Built in October 1905 and withdrawn in March 1963, it arrived at Barry in November 1963 and was taken to the Gloucestershire Warwickshire Railway in June 1981, where it achieved steam in 2010.

Although this loco has 2857 painted on the cylinder block, it is unlikely to be that engine as it was removed from Barry in August 1975. No. 2859, however, has the same date painted on the boiler as it was transported away to Llangollen in October 1987, so it is most probably that engine.

Engulfed in summer greenery, but somehow picturesque. The last Churchward 2800 class to survive Barry was No. 2874 and although this is not that engine, it was clearly marked as a donor for parts to ensure its survival.

The same Churchward locomotive is seen here at a different time of year and location within the yard.

A survivor of the Collett 2884 class 2-8-0, No. 2885 is seen here with the ominous oxyacetylene metal-cutter's kit ready and waiting to start work. Departing Barry in March 1981, it spent ten years as a static display at Birmingham Moor Street station from 2003. It is currently under full restoration at Tyseley.

Collett 2-8-0 No. 3814 was built in March 1940 and withdrawn in December 1964. It arrived at Barry in March 1965 and departed in July 1986 to the North Yorkshire Moors Railway. Work began on restoration in 2018 at Llangollen Engineering but it is now at Northern Steam Engineering in Stockton awaiting completion.

One of the last of the 2884 class to arrive at Barry in October 1965, No. 3850 departed in April 1984 to the West Somerset Railway as their first locomotive. Since achieving steam in 2006 it has successfully covered 82,000 miles of track and is now undergoing overhaul.

Stablemate Collett No. 3855, with the iconic 'Bad day for steam' on its smokebox door, moved from Barry in August 1985, with four other GWR locomotives, to the Pontypool & Blaenavon Railway. Built in 1942, it is finally under restoration at a site in Bury.

The same Collett locomotive and its tender are seen here with the 'Bad' replaced with 'Good' on the smokebox door, probably after the engine was successfully purchased.

Left: A portrait shot of No. 3855 emphasises the extent of vegetation that engulfed many of the locomotives that were sometimes motionless for years after delivery to the yard.

Below: Collett No. 3862 stands silent and alone in the setting sun. The warm orange light picks up on the rust-coated surfaces, giving a sense of the final moments of Woodham's yard as the last of the rescued locomotives made their way quietly out of Barry.

Right: A close-up portrait shot of No. 3862 in which the richness of the ochre tones and earthy highlights add sombre notes to the passing of the golden age.

Below: Collett class 5101 2-6-2T No. 4115 no longer exists. Built in October 1936 and withdrawn in June 1965, it arrived at Barry in August 1965 and departed in March 1988 as one of the last ten locomotives to leave. It was a donor of many significant parts to GWR No. 4709 and was officially scrapped in 2016.

Churchward 4200 class 2-8-0T No. 4247 sits amongst a mixture of rolling stock including a cut-and-shut diesel brake tender. Built in March 1916 and withdrawn in April 1964, it survived over twenty years at Barry before achieving steam again in 2001 at the Bodmin & Wenford Railway. It is currently undergoing an overhaul before returning to Dartmouth Steam Railway.

Classmate No. 4248, built in the same year as No. 4247, left Barry in May 1986 for the Swindon Steam Railway Museum, where it remains today as a conserved partially dismantled locomotive on display.

Another running mate of the Churchward 4200 class, No. 4253 was originally repatriated in August 1987 to the Pontypool & Blaenavon Railway but is now at the Kent & East Sussex Railway, where restoration is nearing completion.

The front end of the same locomotive is seen here in reasonably complete condition at the buffers.

Churchward No. 4277, built in April 1920 and withdrawn in June 1964, arrived three months later in September and waited twenty-two years. Now owned by the Dartmouth Steam Railway, it has the name *Hercules* and is currently back in operation after an overhaul.

Collett 4900 class 4-6-0 No. 4979 *Wootton Hall*, built in February 1930 and withdrawn in December 1963, arrived at Barry in June 1964 and departed in October 1986 to Fleetwood Locomotive Centre. It's now based at Ribble Steam Railway where restoration is underway to make it the largest engine on the line.

Collett 5205 class 2-8-0T No. 5227 was one of the last ten to leave Barry in February 1988, having been moved around the yard for some twenty-five years. It is now a donor engine, with parts going to other GWR locomotives under restoration. What remains is at the Didcot Railway Centre.

Churchward 4575 class 2-6-2T No. 5526, built in May 1928 and withdrawn in June 1962, arrived at Barry in October 1962 and departed to the Gloucestershire Warwickshire Railway in July 1985. The restored locomotive moved to the South Devon Railway where it has been operational, although it is currently on loan to the Gwili Railway.

Churchward 4575 classmate No. 5538 was given to the local council by Woodham's yard with the intention of it being displayed on Barry seafront. After some cosmetic restoration it was on display there from 1992 until 1997. It later moved to the Dean Forest Railway, where parts were swapped with No. 5532, and is under restoration.

One of the 'Barry Ten', No. 5539 spent a further twenty years owned by Vale of Glamorgan Council, which sold it on, it arriving in Llangollen in 2006. It has now moved back to Barry where the Tourist Railway are continuing to restore the locomotive.

One of the many GWR 2-6-2T locos that were unceremoniously dumped in a procession. The engine number has since disappeared and is not formally identified, although it has a plea to be kept as a spare. This may well be one of the sorry few that met its end here at Woodham's yard.

The rotting rusty tail end of No. 5539 is illuminated by the setting sun. Alongside BR Standard No. 44901, they cast a melancholy picture in which you can almost smell the decay creeping through the steel.

Built in November 1928, No. 5552 was moved in June 1986 to the Bodmin & Wenford Railway, where, in 2003, after major restoration works, it became regular traction. Under overhaul from 2012, it is now back in service.

Built in the same month as No. 5552, No. 5553 was taken to the Dean Forest Railway as the longest serving and last locomotive to leave Woodham's yard in January 1990. Pete Waterman returned it to steam in 2002 serving the West Somerset Railway and it is now operational at Peak Rail after a major overhaul.

Collett class 4900 4-6-0 No. 5967 *Bickmarsh Hall*, built in March 1937 and withdrawn in June 1964, arrived at Barry in August 1964 and departed in August 1987 with four other GWR locomotives to the Pontypool & Blaenavon Railway. This photograph clearly demonstrates the chaos of the stripping-out process, with piles of pipework and fittings in the foreground.

The same locomotive *Bickmarsh Hall* pictured some years later with fewer other engines around it and protective coatings applied to some areas. Restoration is ongoing at the Northampton & Lamport Railway.

It has not been possible to make a formal identification of this GWR loco but it is evident that having been sold, some work to stop the decline had been done by painting some of the bodywork.

An end-of-the-line photo that looks like it may have been Churchward No. 5553 waiting to be rescued as the last of the 213 locomotives to have made it out of Barry Island.

Collett 6000 class 4-6-0 No. 6023 *King Edward II*, built in June 1930 and withdrawn in June 1962, arrived at Barry in December 1962 and was transported in December 1984. Partly rebuilt, No. 6023 went to the Didcot Railway Centre for the continuation of the restoration and steamed in 2011. The boiler ticket has now expired and it is awaiting an overhaul.

Collett 5600 class 0-6-2T No. 6686 was one of the 'Barry Ten' that left Woodham's yard in the last days of the scrapyard. It is now ninety-five years old and is slowly being restored at the Barry Tourist Railway.

Hawksworth 6959 class 4-6-0 No. 6984 *Owsden Hall*, built in February 1948 and withdrawn in December 1965, arrived at Barry in February 1966 and departed in October 1986. Initially at the Gloucestershire Warwickshire Railway, it is now at the Buckinghamshire Railway Centre for the remainder of the restoration with a view to achieving steam in 2025.

Owsden Hall seen a few years later with a replaced chimney and some protective paintwork. The grass has encroached a fair bit into the picture too.

This is a shot of the opposite side of No. 6984 *Owsden Hall*, shown complete with its tender.

Another Hawksworth 6959 class 4-6-0, No. 7927 *Willington Hall*, built in October 1950 and withdrawn in December 1965, arrived at Barry in February 1966. *Willington Hall* was used as a donor engine for the No. 1014 *County of Glamorgan* and No. 6880 *Betton Grange* projects.

Above: Collett 5700 class 0-6-0PT No. 9682, built in May 1949 and withdrawn in August 1965, arrived at Barry in October 1965, departing in November 1982. Returning to steam in 2000, it went out on loan to various heritage railway lines. It has since been sold on and is awaiting overhaul at the Dean Forest Railway.

Left: Urie S15 class 4-6-0 No. 30499 was built in May 1920 and withdrawn in January 1964. It arrived at Barry in June 1964 and departed to the Mid-Hants Railway in November 1983. It was a main donor engine for No. 30506 but has since become the focus of its own preservation and it is hoped to see it running in the original LSWR condition.

Maunsell S15 class 4-6-0 No. 30830, built in August 1927 and withdrawn in July 1964, arrived at Barry in December 1964 and departed to the Bluebell Railway in September 1987. It was second in line, behind No. 30847, to be restored, so it was sold on to the North Yorkshire Moors Railway, which is currently working on it.

There's a separate section on the Bulleid Light Pacifics, however, it would be churlish not to include the one with the longest nameplate, Merchant Navy class No. 35006 *Peninsular & Oriental Steam Navigation Company.*

MN No. 35009 *Shaw Savill* waits patiently amongst the chaos and debris of Woodham's yard with BR Standard 5MT No. 73156.

LMS Stanier 5FH class 2-6-0 No. 42859, built in March 1930 and withdrawn in December 1966, arrived at Barry in June 1967 and departed in December 1986. This locomotive has had a troubled time since leaving Woodham's and the future is still uncertain, but it is hoped it will be restored one day.

Stanier No. 42859 from a more trackside perspective through the summer undergrowth. BR Standard 4MT No. 80104 keeps it company.

LMS Fowler 4F 0-6-0 No. 44123, built in July 1925 and withdrawn in June 1965, arrived at Barry in August 1965, departing for the Mid-Hants Railway in December 1981. It is now at the Avon Valley Railway undergoing final restoration with the hope that it will steam again 100 years after being built.

LMS Stanier 5P5F 4-6-0 Black Five No. 45163, built in August 1935 and withdrawn in May 1965, arrived at Barry in January 1966 and departed to the Humberside Locomotive Preservation Group in January 1987. Colne Valley Railway are now in charge of the restoration programme.

A view from the opposite side of No. 45163 showing the seriousness of the twenty years of neglect. It is sitting in a line of Black Fives with No. 45337 for company.

Stanier No. 45163 is looking a bit dishevelled, although this photograph shows the smokebox door and cowling still in place.

LMS Stanier 5P5F 4-6-0 Black Five No. 45293, built in December 1936 and withdrawn in August 1965, arrived at Barry in January 1966 and departed to the British Enginemen Steam Preservation Society in December 1986. Colne Valley Railway are now in charge of the restoration programme.

LMS Stanier 5P5F 4-6-0 Black Five No. 45337, built in April 1937 and withdrawn in February 1965, arrived at Barry in January 1966 and departed in May 1984. It was restored by East Lancashire Railway and steamed again in 1995, going out on loan to various heritage railways. A second overhaul is underway and it will return to traffic as soon as possible.

LMS Fowler 3F Jinty 0-6-0 No. 47406, built in November 1926 and withdrawn in December 1966, arrived at Barry in June 1967 and departed to Peak Rail (originally at Buxton). It moved to the Great Central Railway in 1989 and achieved steam in 2010. HRH King Charles III drove this engine in January 2017 and it's currently awaiting an overhaul.

A later shot of Jinty No. 47406 with the faded British Railways crest just visible on the tank where grass is growing out of the top.

The classic end-of-the-line shot with two of the workhorses of the railways. On the left, LMS Stanier 8F 2-8-0 No. 48173, built in July 1943 and withdrawn in July 1965, arrived at Barry in October 1965 and departed in September 1988. It was bought by the Avon Valley Railway, and is now owned and being restored at Churnet Valley Railway.

A slightly later picture of the same locomotives. On the right BR Standard 4MT 2-6-0 No. 76084, built in April 1957 and withdrawn in December 1967, arrived at Barry in September 1968 and departed in March 1983. It is looking particularly weather-beaten with the words 'Burnley Pufter' painted on the buffer beam above 'Lower Darwen'. It is now under restoration at the Gloucestershire Warwickshire Railway.

LMS Stanier 8F 2-8-0 No. 48305, built in November 1943 and withdrawn in January 1968, arrived at Barry in September 1968 and departed in November 1985, having been saved by Roger Hibbert. 'Please don't let me die' was transported to the Great Central Railway, where it achieved steam in 1995 and entered traffic. It has since had two ten-year overhauls and is operational once more.

Stanier 8F No. 48305, seen here a few years later when some of the stock has been moved, rescued or dismantled and a full-length side shot can now be taken, somewhat unusually complete with a tender.

Sister LMS Stanier 8F No. 48624, built in December 1943 and withdrawn in July 1965, arrived at Barry in October 1965 and departed to the Severn Valley Railway in July 1981. Bought by the '48624 group', it underwent twenty-eight years of restoration (mostly outdoors) before achieving steam in 2009 at Peak Rail. It is awaiting overhaul at the Great Central Railway.

BR Standard 5MT 4-6-0 No. 73096, built in December 1956 and withdrawn in November 1967, arrived at Barry in February 1968 and departed in July 1985 to the Mid-Hants Railway, where it was fully restored in 1993. It worked main-line services and then suffered serious cylinder damage whilst working at the Mid-Hants. It is now awaiting major overhaul.

Classmate 5MT No. 73156 departed Barry in October 1986 to the East Lancashire Railway. Built and withdrawn at the same time as No. 73096, it achieved steam and moved under its own effort in 2017, and after a couple of mechanical adjustments it entered traffic at the Great Central Railway in 2018.

BR Standard 4MT 4-6-0 No. 75079, built in January 1956 and withdrawn in November 1966, arrived at Barry in April 1967 and departed to the Plym Valley Railway in March 1982. Working its entire life on the Southern Region, it is now at the Mid-Hants Railway where restoration is underway with hopes to achieve steam in 2025.

BR Standard 4MT 2-6-0 No. 76077, built in December 1956 and withdrawn in December 1967, arrived at Barry in September 1968 and departed in May 1987 to Toddington on the Gloucestershire Warwickshire Railway, where it is continuing its journey towards restoration and achieving full steam.

Left: BR Standard 2MT 2-6-0 No. 78059, built in September 1956 and withdrawn in September 1966, arrived at Barry in June 1966 and departed to the Bluebell Railway in May 1983. The intention is to use No. 78059 as a donor engine for the 84030 project (which is currently underway) because none of the tanked 2MT versions survived the Beeching (or Woodham) cuts.

Below: BR Standard 4MT 2-6-4T No. 80072, built in November 1953 and withdrawn in July 1965, arrived at Barry in January 1966 and departed in July 1988. Cutting a despondent silhouette of rust with the skyline of Barry town in the background, No 80072 was returned to steam in 2009 at the Llangollen Railway and is now being overhauled.

Viewed from the opposite corner, the devastation of parts cannibalism and weathering is evident on No. 80072 ,the 206th locomotive to be liberated from Woodham's yard.

Another BR Standard 4MT (believed to be No. 80078) sits in amongst a line of condemned locomotives and the high grass and vegetation of late summer 1981.

BR Standard 4MT 2-6-4T No. 80098, built in December 1954 and withdrawn in July 1965, arrived at Barry in January 1966 and departed to the Midland Railway in November 1984. It steamed again in August 1998, obtaining a main-line certificate. Now the boiler certificate has expired it is undergoing heavy overhaul.

BR Standard 4MT 2-6-4T No. 80104, built in March 1955 and withdrawn in July 1965, arrived at Barry with ten others of its class in January 1966. Originally bought by the Southern Steam Trust, it departed in September 1984 and stood on display at Swanage Railway. It moved under its own steam for the first time in April 1997.

The opposite side of No. 80104. Much of the surface looks relatively good in this picture but a great deal of parts have already been removed by others. Now owned by Southern Locomotives Ltd, it is under heavy overhaul at Tyseley.

The last example of the tanked 4MT to leave Barry as one of the 'Ten' rescued at the last minute. It looks in a very sorry state here and sadly it is unlikely to be fully restored as years of weathering have made it unviable. It is hoped to have No. 80150 as a display locomotive at its Mid-Hants home.

BR Standard 9F 2-10-0 No. 92207, built in June 1959 and withdrawn in December 1964, arrived at Barry in March 1965 and departed to the East Lancashire Railway in October 1986. Part restoration eventually saw it bought and relocated to the Somerset & Dorset Railway Heritage Trust site at Shillingstone, where the work will continue once funds have been secured.

BR Standard 9F No. 92219, built in January 1960, saw only five-and-a-half years of traffic before withdrawal and despatch to Barry. Initially transported to Peak Rail in May 1985, a lack of funding has meant that only partial restoration has taken place and although it is now at Strathspey and under cover, it is still in scrapyard condition.

This 9F (No. 92245) was one of the 'Barry Ten' to be taken to the Vale of Glamorgan yard in February 1988. It is still part of the Barry Tourist Railway, although the boiler and cab are in other locations. It will form part of the scrapyard experience.

Not everything that went into Dai Woodham's yard was a steam engine; indeed anything that was condemned or withdrawn by BR within a given geographical area might have been sent here to be recycled, and the diesels that were to replace steam locomotion were no exception. An early shunter rots in line with rolling stock, cheek by jowl with BB class No. 34073 *249 Squadron*.

Left: 2884 class GWR Collett 2-8-0 No. 3855 displays the encroaching vegetation and the sad handwritten reality that faced the steam preservation societies of the day. The Pontypool & Blaenavon Railway saved this one.

Below: A view from within the smokebox. The chains add an ominous mood to the demise of the casing.

No. 6023 *King Edward II*'s torch-cut driving wheel. *Galatea* suffered the same fate after a derailment meant that lifting was not an option when the loco needed to be moved.

Another cut wheel on the pony truck of what looks like BR Standard 4MT No. 80072. This one was clearly earmarked for Brighton works.

Above: A framed shot of the cylinders and what remains of the connecting gear on a BR Standard.

Left: Nature is gradually taking over in all the nooks and crannies of these sleeping giants as they quietly rust away in the salty air of South Wales.

Built in 1920, Urie S15 class 4-6-0 No. 30499 has either been stripped down to the main frame and wheels, or this is the donor locomotive for No. 30499, which was bought by the Urie Preservation Society.

This sunset-lit tender, in not too bad condition, was reserved for GWR 4900 class Collett No. 4979 *Wootton Hall*, which initially moved to Fleetwood in Lancashire in 1986.

A solitary tender from Guildford that had been converted into a water tank has been condemned and awaits its fate amongst the piles of scrap.

Carriage wheels are crudely cut from their axles and are then piled up like matchsticks in amongst the rampant buddleia.

So much rolling stock was taken to Woodham's yard for scrap, not just the locomotives. Here a line of identical part-wood and part-metal brake vans is in the process of being dismantled.

A rail winch wagon sitting in amongst the lines of condemned hopper wagons.

Above: Looking into a brake van where partial dilapidation has started the process of dismantling this unit.

Left: A driver's eye view along the boiler and down the line of wagons.

Right: The view from the other side of the cab looking down the adjacent line to Stanier Black Five 4-6-0 No. 45293.

Below: One of the later views from the footplate looking towards the fenced-off end of the tracks. GWR Collett No. 4115 and Churchward No. 5539 are waiting for their turn to be rescued.

An interesting picture of the erosion that revealed the various formats of regional (Southern) and national (British Railways) identification on this tender. This is most likely Maunsell S15 4-6-0 No. 30847, which moved from Barry in 1978 and achieved steam in 1992.

A curious fish-eye lens shot between the last few remaining locos and vans. Stanier 8F 2-8-0 No. 48173 departed in September 1988 as the 208th to be rescued and initially went to the Avon Valley Railway.

A view of the demise on the footplate and cab of MN No. 35009 *Shaw Savill*. It's almost as if the firebox is screaming for coal!

There's a lovely build-up of depth here, from the unseen wagons in the foreground and the lines of locomotives to the storage tanks and then the buildings beyond. Hawksworth No.7927 *Willington Hall* sits nose to nose with a Bulleid Light Pacific.

Churchward 2-6-2T No. 5552 spent twenty-five years in the sidings before leaving Barry. It's back to back here with one of the other 100 GWR locomotive brought to Barry to be scrapped but rescued one way or another.

The church that is visible through the cab of BR Standard 9F No. 92245 has no doubt been witness to many happenings in Barry, the least of which is the mere six years of traction this amazing locomotive gave to the railways. It never left South Wales and remains at the Barry Tourist Railway.

Various stages of decay are visible in this shot. BR Standard 4MT No. 80097 made it out of Barry in 1985 and has since been fully restored to steam at the East Lancashire Railway.

The light in this picture really emphasises the patina and delamination of the two locomotives. MN No. 35027 rests back to back with BR Standard 4MT No. 76077, both without their tenders.

Left: In between the slowly rotting stock of locomotives, vans and wagons is a cut con' rod lying on the ground.

Below: A ground-level portrait shot up through the invasive buddleia and silhouettes and shadows of the loco lines.

Above: Cross-loco straddling here! A typical view down the seemingly never-ending lines of engines before many of them had been repatriated.

Right: Collett 2-8-0 No. 3802 and Churchward 2-8-0T No. 4247, both reserved and enjoying the Welsh afternoon sun before parting in 1984 and 1985, respectively.

Sparks still flying around the yard as the cutter's torch gets to work on a pile of rails, which, along with the wagons, kept Woodham's in business after loco cutting ceased in the early 1980s.

WC class Bulleid Light Pacific No. 34028 *Eddystone*, built in May 1946 and withdrawn in May 1964, arrived at Barry in November 1964 and departed in May 1986. It is currently operating on the Swanage Railway having been rescued by the Southern Pacific Rescue group, which took it to Sellindge, near Ashford, for restoration.

WC class Bulleid Light Pacific No. 34046 *Braunton*, built in November 1946 and withdrawn in October 1965, arrived at Barry in January 1966 and departed July 1988. It was taken to the Brighton Locomotive Works before being bought by the West Somerset Railway for restoration, making it back to steam in 2007.

Another view of *Braunton* that shows the extent of the dilapidation not long before it moved. There are a lot of parts missing that inevitably ended up on sister locomotives.

A silhouetted shot of *Braunton* from the opposite corner. The cylinder has 34027 (Taw Valley) painted on it. Whether that was by consent only a few will know but that engine is currently at the Severn Valley Railway.

A final view of No. 34046 not long before it was shipped out from Woodham's yard – the writing on the cylinder appears to have been 'Tipp-Exed'. It returned to steam in 2020 at Crewe, its current home base.

Right: BB class Bulleid Light Pacific No. 34053 *Sir Keith Park*, built in January 1947 and withdrawn in October 1965, arrived at Barry in March 1966 and departed in June 1984. Not the easiest shot of this iconically named loco but unmistakeable with its number painted on the side. It is currently owned by Southern Locomotives Ltd and under restoration at Herston.

Below: BB class Bulleid Light Pacific No. 34070 *Manston*, built in November 1947 and withdrawn in August 1964, arrived at Barry in December 1964 and departed in June 1983. Looking in poor shape with a tarpaulin over the smokebox, *Manston*, owned by Southern Locomotives Ltd, is now fully restored and operating on the Swanage Railway.

BB class Bulleid Light Pacific No. 34072 *257 Squadron*, built in April 1948 and withdrawn in October 1964, arrived at Barry in March 1965 and departed in November 1984. With much of its air-smoothing bodywork missing in this picture, a nearly fully restored engine will be operating on the Spa Valley Railway in the future; it is owned by Southern Locomotives Ltd.

MN class Bulleid Light Pacific No. 35006 *Peninsular & Oriental Steam Navigation Company*, built in December 1941 and withdrawn in August 1964, arrived at Barry in December 1964 and departed in March 1983. Returning to traffic some fifty years after withdrawal from service, No. 35006 now operates on the Gloucestershire Warwickshire Railway.

MN class Bulleid Light Pacific No. 35009 *Shaw Savill*, built in June 1942 and withdrawn in September 1964, arrived at Barry in December 1964 and departed in February 1989. Still under a restoration programme at Ian Riley engineering, the plan is to return No. 35009 to main-line service.

MN class Bullied Light Pacific No. 35010 *Blue Star*, built in July 1942 and withdrawn in September 1966, arrived at Barry in March 1967 and departed in January 1985. Shunted right up against No. 34072 and with its wheel rims painted white in this picture, *Blue Star* now resides at Colne Valley Railway awaiting its turn to be restored.

Above: An earlier picture of No. 35010 in colour showing a clearer view into the smokebox and note the brake connecting rods are still intact.

Left: A detailed picture of *Blue Star* showing where the nameplate would have been, lovingly painted in by one of the rescue group's members.

Above: MN class Bulleid Light Pacific No. 35011 *General Steam Navigation*, built in December 1944 and withdrawn in February 1966, arrived at Barry in June 1966 and departed in March 1989. No. 35011 is now in the hands of a private preservation society and is based at the Swindon & Cricklade Railway, where it waits until extensive work can be carried out.

Right: One of the many front-end shots of GSN, a locomotive that covered over a million track miles in its short service history.

Standing alone as the last Bulleid to be moved from Woodham's yard, No. 35011 looks forlorn but ready to be transported to Preston Park, Brighton.

MN class Bulleid Light Pacific No. 35022 *Holland America Line*, built in October 1948 and withdrawn in May 1966, arrived at Barry in November 1966 and departed in March 1986. Originally purchased in 1983 by the Southern Steam Trust, No. 35022 is now under the ownership of the Royal Scot Locomotive and General Trust and remains in storage at Crewe.

A close-up line-side view of the driving wheels of No. 35022, which covered railway metals as far afield as Carlisle.

MN class Bulleid Light Pacific No. 35025 *Brocklebank Line*, built in November 1948 and withdrawn in September 1964, arrived at Barry in December 1964 and departed in February 1986. Reprieved from the cutter's torch, a late purchase of No. 35025 rescued the loco. The smokebox door was buckled in a shunting incident at the yard. Southern Locomotives are planning to restore the loco.

MN class Bulleid Light Pacific No. 35027 *Port Line*, built in December 1948 and withdrawn in September 1966, arrived at Barry in March 1967 and departed in December 1982. The first MN class to achieve steam in 1988 after restoration, *Port Line* spent some time at Swanage Railway from 2000 to 2003. It is owned by the Royal Scot Locomotive and General Trust and awaiting overhaul at Crewe.

Collett class 2884 2-8-0 No. 3855 in summer 1982. What a difference a grey makes! A coat of anti-rust primer helps stop further ravages from the elements in the open yard. Arriving at Barry in 1965 and departing in 1987 for the Pontypool & Blaenavon Railway, it is currently at the East Lancs Railway undergoing total restoration.

Collett class 5700 0-6-0 tank No. 9682 is seen in August 1980. Built in 1949 and sent to Woodham's in 1965, it left in 1982. Returned to steam in 2000 by GWR Southall, it worked several heritage railways until 2009. During overhaul in 2018, £35,000 of its parts were stolen. No. 9682 is now owned by the Dean Forest Railway, where it awaits restoration.

A study in silhouette. Two unidentified GWR Churchward 2-8-0 locos appear nose to nose, but on adjacent tracks. The potential for 'artistic' photos at Barry was considerable, especially when using black-and-white film. I rarely failed to note numbers, but these slipped through the net. Where are they now?

Above: Looking good with its black paint job, Churchward 2-8-0 T No. 4277 was built in 1920 and arrived at Barry in 1964, concluding a lifetime in South Wales. Privately purchased in 1986, it was then sold to the Dartmouth Railway in 2008, where it was re-steamed and named *Hercules*. Majorly overhauled from 2018 until 2021, it then returned to service.

Left: Sporting a splendid rain hat, Collett class 2884 2-8-0 No. 3803 was built in 1939. Withdrawn in 1963 and sent to Woodham's, it spent its final working years attached to Severn Tunnel Junction, a few miles east of Barry. No. 3803 left the scrapyard in 1983 for the South Devon Railway, Buckfastleigh. Re-steamed in 2005, it is owned by Dartmouth Steam Railway.

A 1981 photographic contrast of the same loco – firstly black and white. Originally constructed as 2-8-0T No. 5275, it was rebuilt in 1934 as a 2-8-2T and renumbered 7200. It is one of only four locomotives to have the coal-scuttle bunker, which gave it greater water-carrying capacity for longer distances.

Now colour. Withdrawn in 1963 and sold to Woodham's, it remained until 1981. It was purchased by the Quainton Road Society in Buckinghamshire, the precise date of which can clearly be seen. Currently nearing the end of several years of major restoration, the return to steam of this unique loco is eagerly anticipated.

GWR 4-6-0 No. 7903 *Foremarke Hall* was built in 1949, one of 259 in the Hall class. Withdrawn to Woodham's in 1964 and sold to the Swindon & Cricklade Railway in 1981, restoration was completed in 2003 when it moved to the Gloucestershire Warwickshire Railway, where it operates today under the ownership of The Foremarke Hall Group.

Barry stablemate GWR No. 5952 *Cogan Hall* was built in 1935 and sold to Woodham's in 1964, sitting with No. 7903 for seventeen years. Privately purchased in 1981 by the Gloucestershire Warwickshire Railway, it moved via Llangollen, Oswestry and Llynclys until 2010, when bought for parts by the Betton Grange Society, which was planning a loco new build.

Almost ready for the off. No. 5952 looking quite superb from the other side in GWR green and red oxide. It has already supplied parts for the building of 'the loco that never was', No. 6880 *Betton Grange*, an impressive project underway at the Tyseley loco works, although restoration is also a possibility.

GWR 4-6-0 No. 6023 *King Edward II* was built in 1930 and withdrawn to Woodham's in 1962. It was coupled to its twin, No. 6024 *King Edward I*, until that departed in 1974. No. 6023 had its driving wheels cut after a yard derailment and stayed until 1985. Completely rebuilt by the Great Western Society at Didcot, it re-steamed in 2011.

GWR 4-6-0 No. 4953 *Pitchford Hall* (minus tender) was built in 1929 and withdrawn in 1963. It was the 150th loco to leave Woodham's in 1984. It was privately purchased and restored at Tyseley, re-steaming in 2004. Following time at the Great Central Railway, it was resold in 2011 and moved to the Epping Ongar Railway. In 2022 it was reportedly for sale again.

An alternate view of GWR 4-6-0 No. 6023 *King Edward II*, the torched driving wheels being on this left side. Once deemed 'project impossible' because of such extensive damage, the full restoration was an engineering landmark. Even here at Barry, No. 6023 was easily the smartest-looking loco in the yard.

I think 15 July 1981 was probably my most memorable day at Barry. After all the previous visits, it was exciting to actually be there on the day a loco was removed for rescue. The loco was LMS Black Five 4-6-0 No. 45491. I could not believe my luck, so I took a sequence of departure photographs.

Built in 1943 at Derby, No. 45491 spent much it its working life in Scotland and the North of England. It was withdrawn and bought by Woodham's in July 1965. Mike Lawrence Heavy Haulage of Burnham-on-Sea was the go-to for Barry removals, seen here gently shunting the loco into place.

Left: Mike's custom-built low loader had a section of rail track built in, so after getting No. 45491 in the correct place, he reversed his mighty rig up to the open cab and attached a cable to begin the pull. Here he makes some final checks before starting the 72-ton haul.

Below: As the pull began, I was a bit concerned as No. 45491 listed slightly left when coming off the ramp and onto the loader. To have it fall into that pile of wheels would have been quite a problem. However, from his place on the winch, Mike was clearly totally unperturbed.

The wheel's-eye view. No. 45491 is almost aboard, with just the front leading wheels to go. Even in this condition, the power of the loco was evident, as was the number of missing parts and the huge restoration awaiting. I obtained Mike's permission to get so up close and personal.

This could so easily have been the fate of No. 45491. Loaded up and ready to leave, the bread-and-butter wagon-cutting work of Woodham's yard continues unabated. My ears were still ringing from the noise of that huge piece falling to the ground (I wish I'd got his name).

Next time you have a problem reversing into a space, imagine what this was like. Mike had to slowly push that massive load back down to where someone is seen standing in order to access the road out of Woodham's. I only recently noticed his truck was also left-hand drive!

This way to Blackpool. Manoeuvring completed, No. 45491, rescued by the West Lancashire Black Five Society, heads to the ICI works at Hillhouse, then to the Fleetwood Steam Centre, where, sadly, thieves removed some major parts. At the Great Central Railway since 2011, after sixty years a re-steam is imminent.

Our Woodham's visits were always family events, so we all appear in this section. This photograph, taken by my wife, Ann, in black and white, is of me taking one in colour. I love how she framed it. (My co-author David wanted this one in.)

Silly I know, but if you see an open smokebox, you have to get in. I was so much younger then – I'm older than that now. (With apologies to Bob Dylan.)

I might have a problem attempting that today. This is Merchant Navy 4-6-2 No. 35022 *Holland America Line*. No, it isn't one of the girls inside, that's my feet!

Great colours on a summer's day and the wagons keep on coming. I presume Ann had to clamber up to capture this, 'standing on the shoulders of giants', or the cab of Stanier 8F 2-8-0 No. 48173.

And here she is, my wife, Ann, all wrapped up after leaving the cosy wood-burner inside. The collective noun? A 'brake' of guard vans.

Woodham's in winter, hence the anorak, scarf and cap. I was simply taking photos, but many people would be there working on locos, in all weathers. MN No. 35011 *General Steam Navigation* was still waiting.

My childhood dream – on a footplate, hammering along, leaning out of the window, smoke and ash in my eyes. Ready to move to Llangollen in 1981, Collett 4-6-0 *Cogan Hall* is looking resplendent.

My youngest daughter, Wendy (eight), climbing aboard a very smart GWR 0-6-0T, No. 6634, looking like the departure whistle was imminent. This photo was taken just a month after it was reserved and on 25 March 1981 this changed to 'sold and paid for' (by record producer Pete Waterman), departing that June.

The same day and Wendy again, with GWR 0-6-0-T No. 4612. She loved getting in and out of cabs! Forty years later and living in Dorset with children of her own, they would ride on the Swanage Railway, hauled by the loco sitting behind here, BB class No. 34072 *257 Squadron*.

Sean arrived in 1981, and we thought he was never taken there, but I'm holding him at nine months old, with his sisters Jane (sixteen, below), Nicola (thirteen, 'Ra-Ra' skirt) and Wendy (ten, on top). The photo was taken by their mum. 2-8-0T No. 4253 is now at the Kent & East Sussex Railway.

Bibliography and Sources

Beckett, Martin, *The Barry Story* (Southampton: Kingfisher Railway Productions, 1982)

Hardingham, Roger, *The Barry List*, 8th and final edn (Huddersfield: Amadeus Press, 1993)

Nicholson, Peter, *The Barry Album* (Cheltenham: self-published, 1981)

Pigott, Nick, Howard Johnston and Steve Worrall (compiled by), 'The Complete Barry Record' (*Steam Railway Magazine* supplement, 1990)

www.greatwestern.org.uk/barry1 – internet resource and reference

www.preservedbritishsteamlocomotives.com – open access Wordpress website and database pbslocos@gmail.com

Geoff Barker's personal slides, photos, notes and recollections

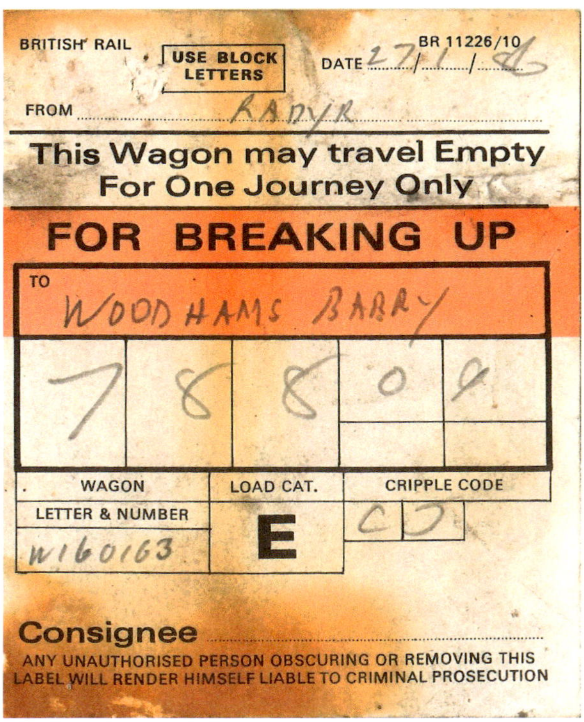

BRITISH RAIL

USE BLOCK LETTERS

BR 11226/10

DATE 27/1/86

FROM RADYR

This Wagon may travel Empty
For One Journey Only

FOR BREAKING UP

TO WOODHAMS BARRY

7 8 8 0 9

WAGON LETTER & NUMBER	LOAD CAT.	CRIPPLE CODE
W160163	E	CJ

Consignee

ANY UNAUTHORISED PERSON OBSCURING OR REMOVING THIS LABEL WILL RENDER HIMSELF LIABLE TO CRIMINAL PROSECUTION

I saved a few souvenirs from the yard: a wooden rail block, an old glove from a cab and one of the cards clipped to wagons sent for cutting. This wagon made the trip from Radyr via Cardiff, Penarth and Barry (a journey still possible today) to its doom in Woodham's yard.